Contents

Score. 5

Alto Sax Part. 9

Piano Part. 10

Bass Part. 12

Drum Set Part. 13

Piano Reduction. 14

Composed in 2021, The Yard Cat Song is the first song I composed after a 10 year hiatus. During my teens, I recall hearing Lee Morgan's original compositions on Philadelphia's WRTI. The songs that I recall were Sidewinder, The Procrastinator, and a few other original tunes. His songs were different from other Bebop musicians in that they had a melody rather than a meandering line of eighth notes. And had a distinct melodic and tonal character lacking in most Bebop compositions.

After not composing or performing for 10 years, I wanted to do something simple yet still had my style imbued upon it. The Yard Cat Song was my attempt to translate a cat's movement atop a fence, in the hopes of catching a bird, only for it to fall off the fence to shake it's head as though nothing happened. Another aspect of this song is the harmonic usage, the first four bars utilize a Lydian cadence, while the second stanza uses an ascending dominant seventh chord progression, and it concludes with pentatonic scale fragments.

And the cat that was the inspiration for this song . . . I haven't seen it in a long time. But then again, looking at how fat it was the last time I saw it . . . perhaps it went on a much needed diet.

Title - The Yard Cat Song
ISBN 13 - 9781955144025
Composer - Andrew T Hanna
Graphic Design, Layout, & Artwork - Andrew T Hanna
Copyright 2021
Genre - Jazz/Bebop/Post-Bop

The Yard Cat Song

Andrew T. Hanna

Solo Section

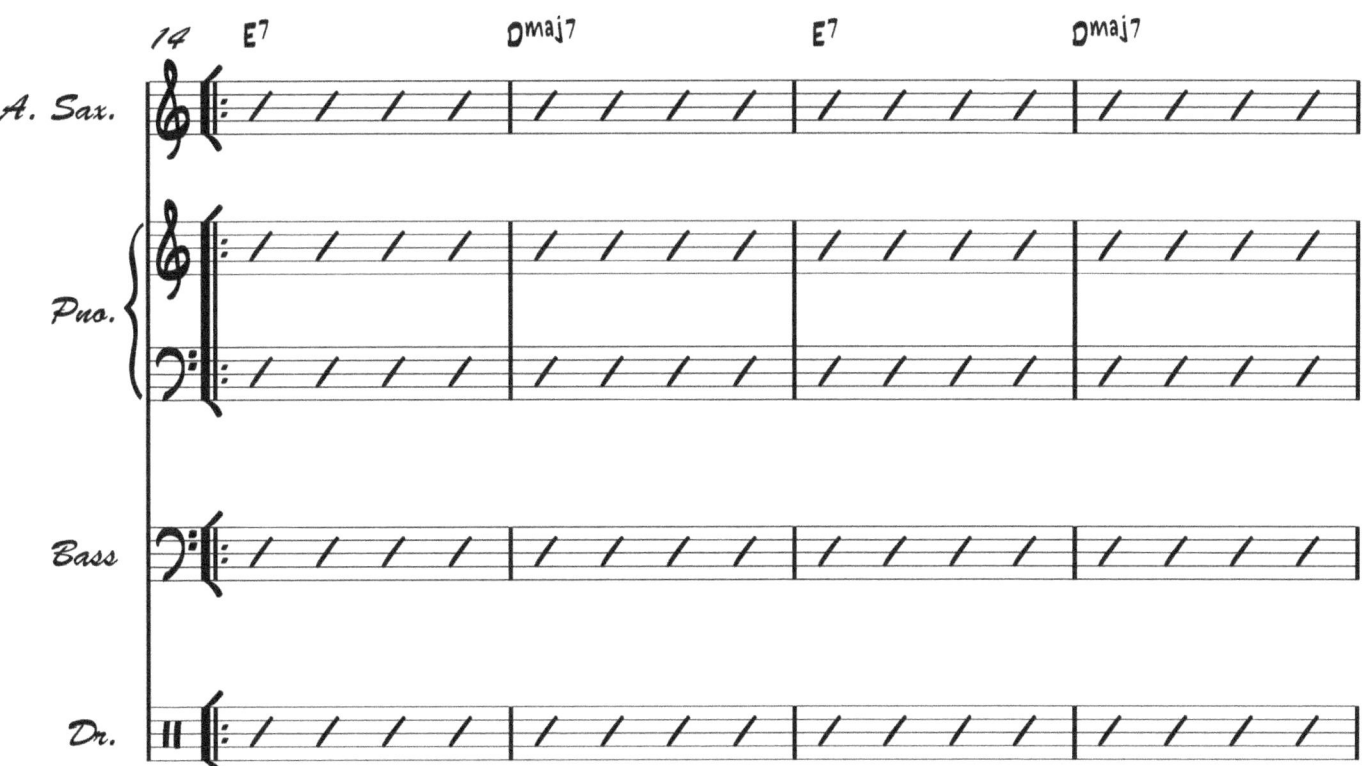

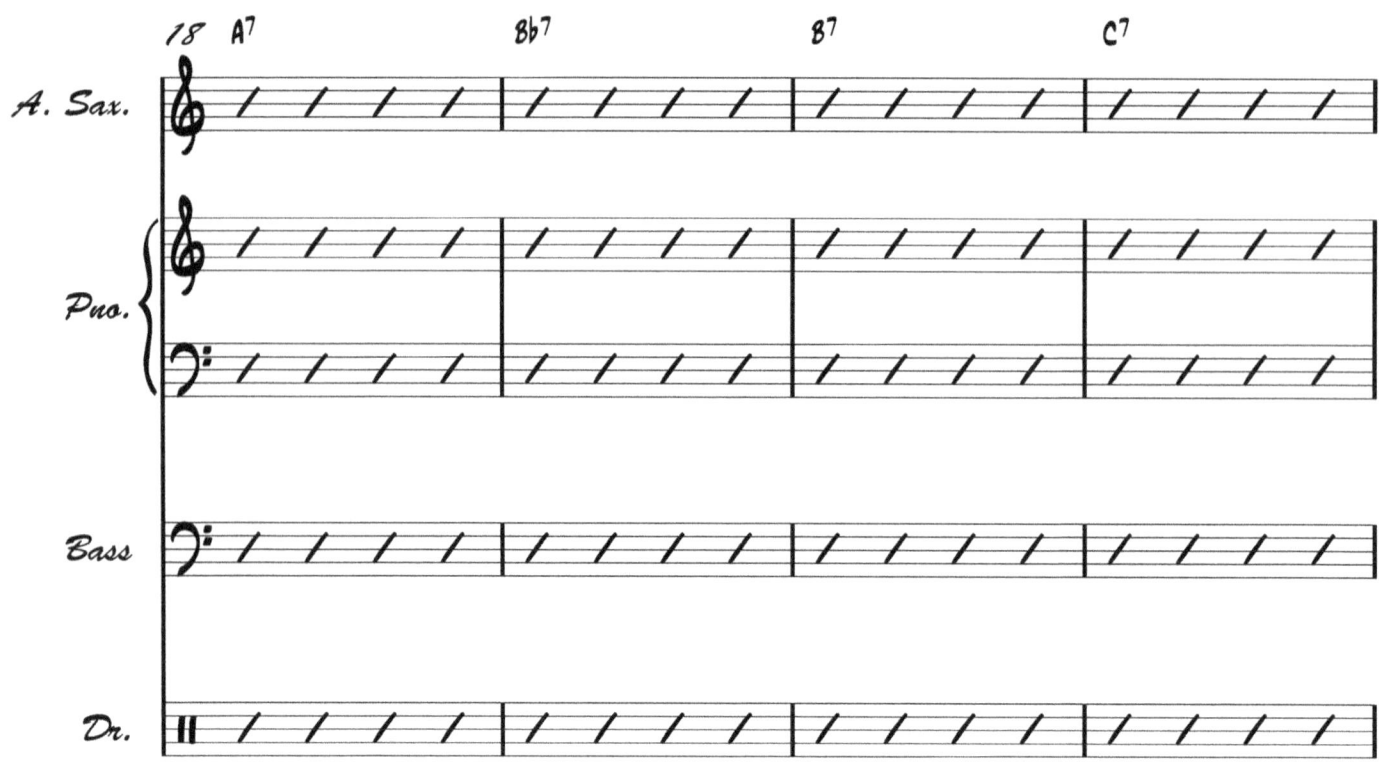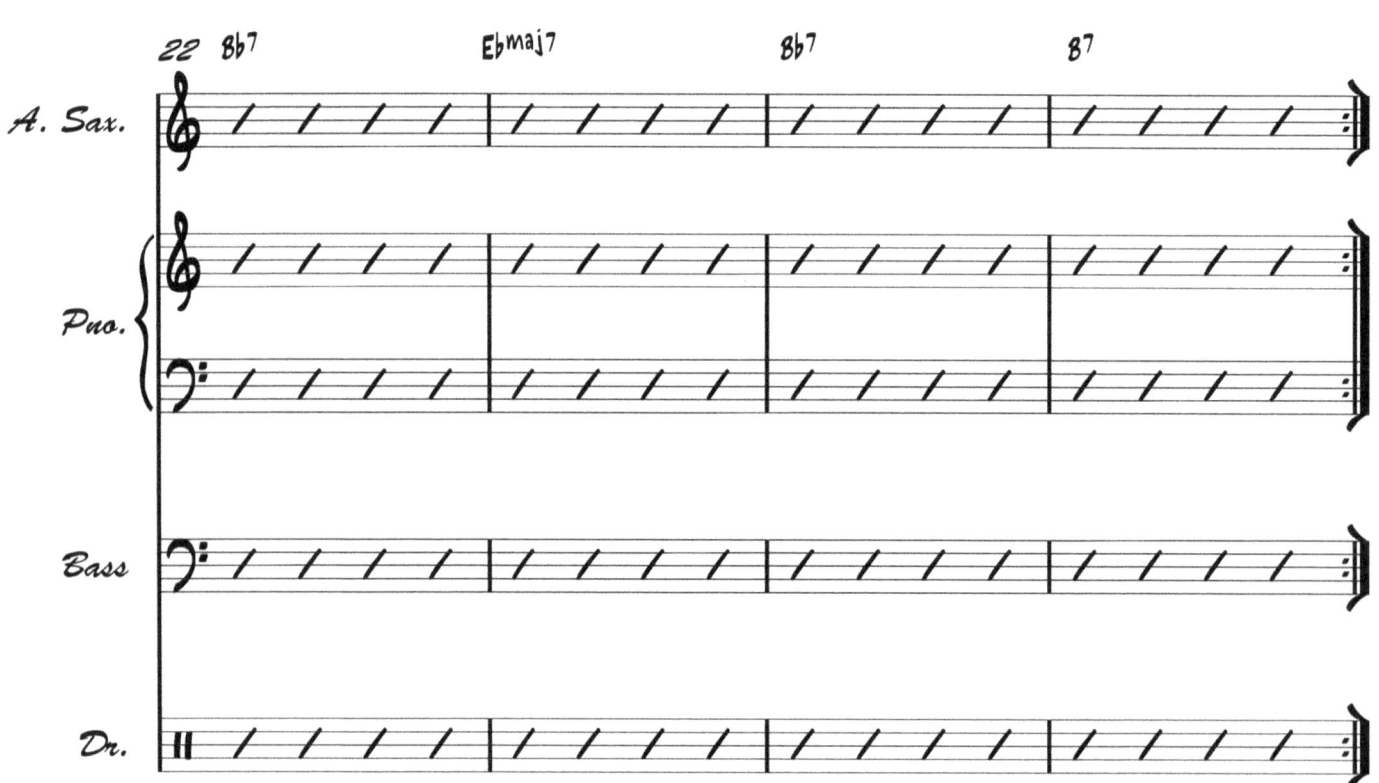

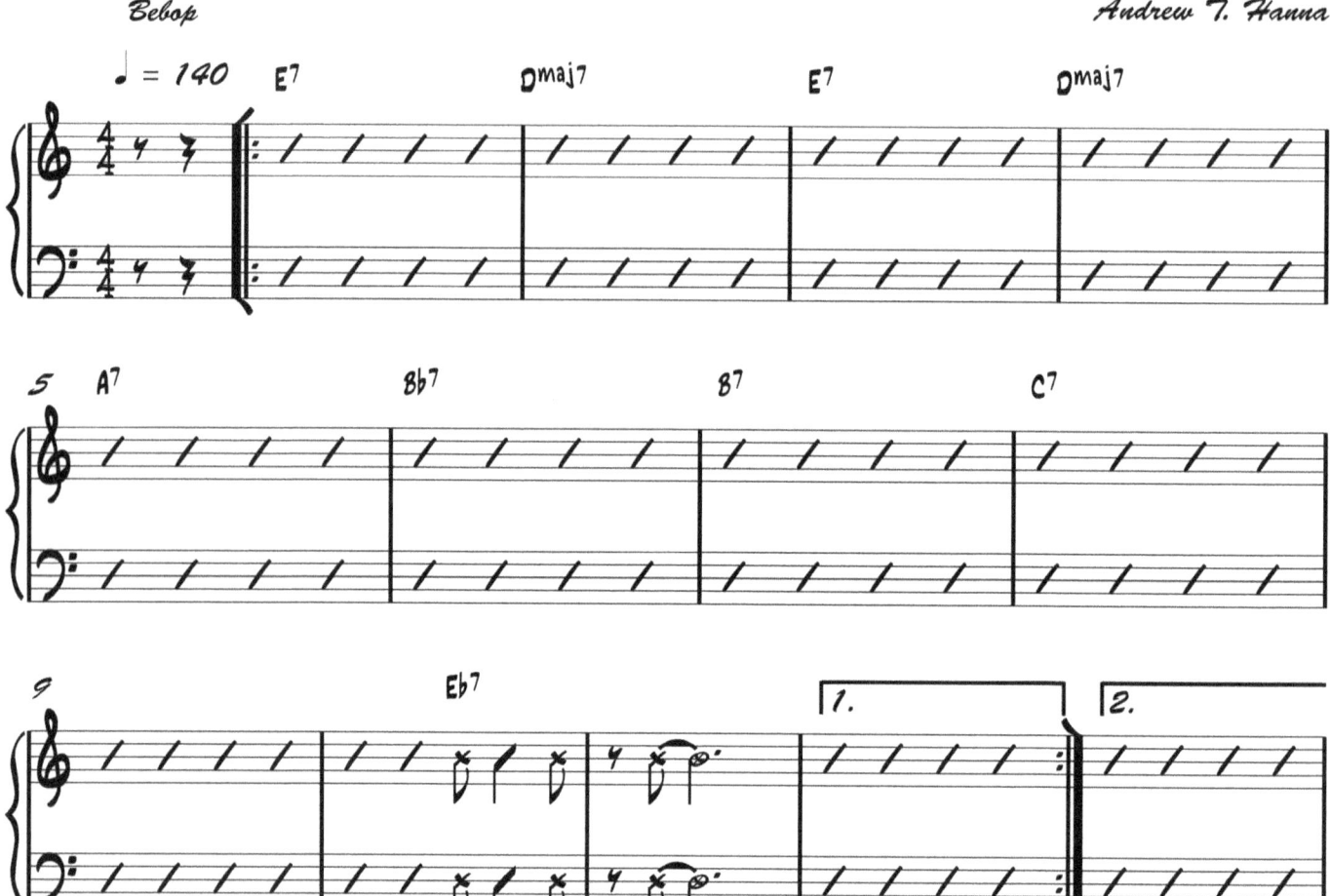

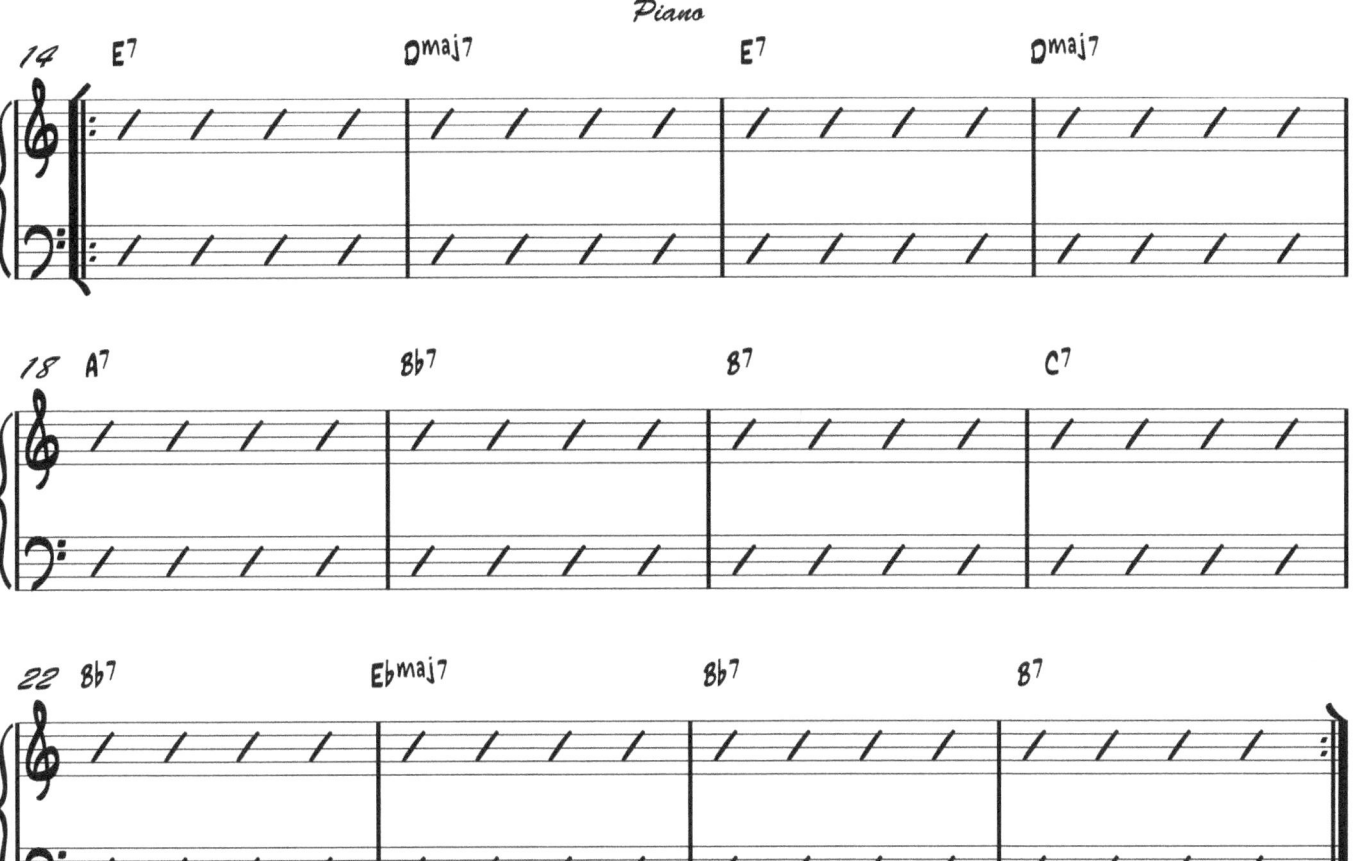

The Yard Cat Song

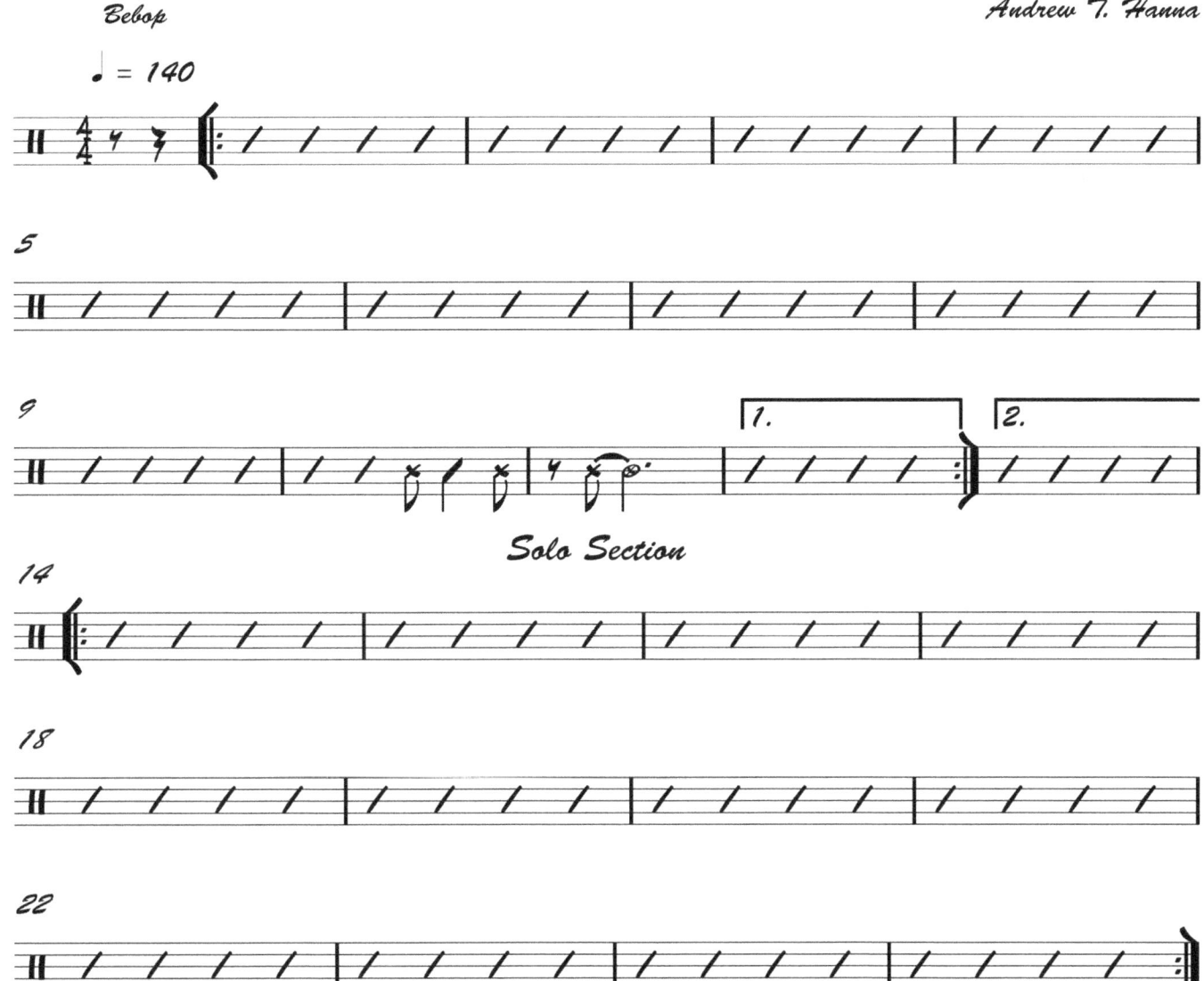

The Yard Cat Song
(Piano Reduction)

Andrew T. Hanna

Bebop

Solo Section

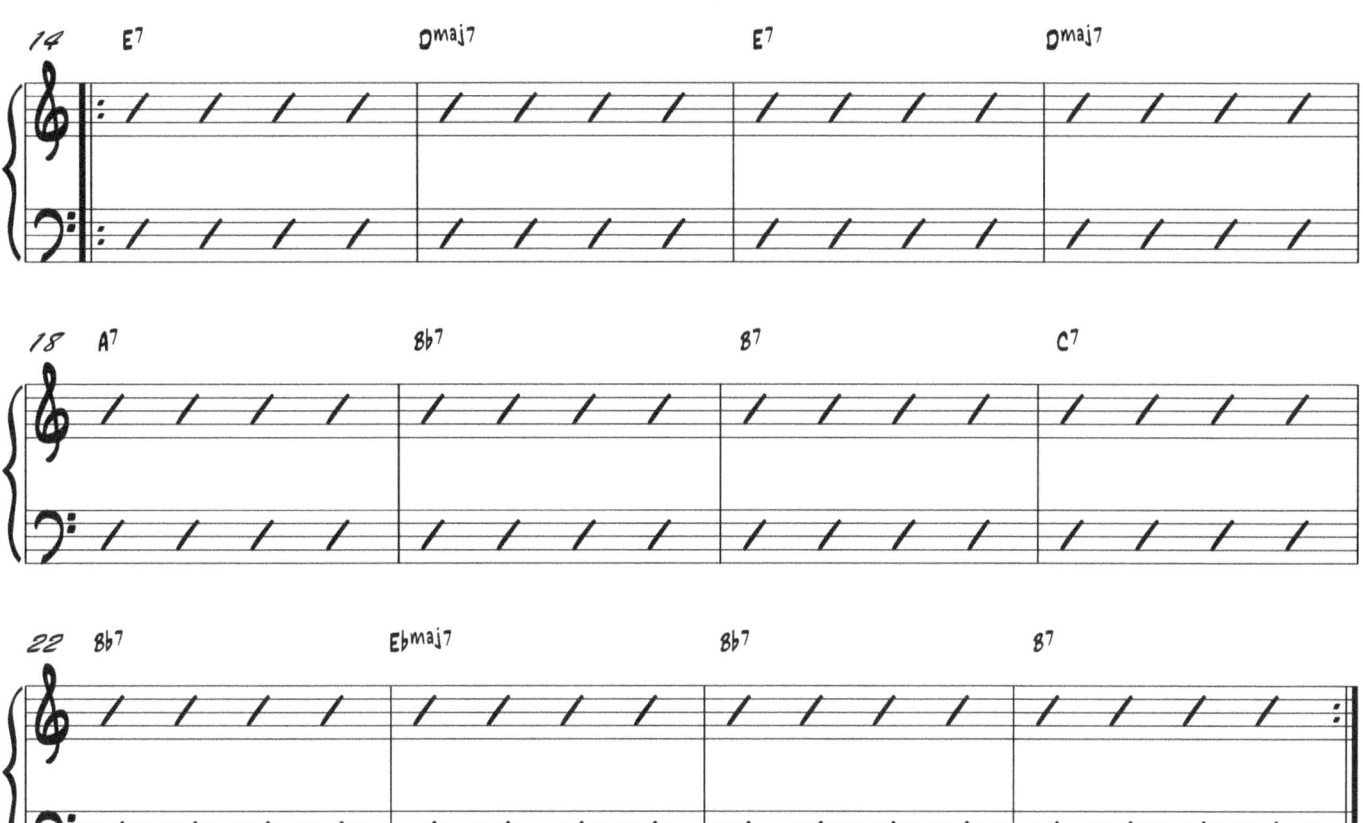